"In this small book are two ma brance of several life-altering exp author began in Seoul, South K part tirade, part profound reflection on our view of men, masculinity, sexuality, and romance. You cannot stop until finished because there is no midway, no stopping point as you become a part of his world. After nearly every sentence you scream with or at his observations either with critical reflections or ecstasy. Ross has his pulse on his generation and the most precarious issues confronting sexuality and romance."

Dr. Ritch C. Savin-Williams, Ph.D., Cornell University
Author of "Mostly Straight: Sexual Fluidity among Men"

"Ross's exploration of sexuality and spirituality is a breath of fresh air in a world full of oppression and discrimination. His writing will have you on the edge of your seat anticipating what comes next. His courage and vulnerability come across on every page, which challenges you to explore your own."

Dr. Kristie Overstreet Ph.D., LPCC, CST
Psychotherapist & Host of Fix Yourself First Podcast

"In talking about his love(s), loss, and the consequences of avoiding pain, Panorama is a soul-baring look at how one man reckons with identity and healing past wounds...Victory's positioning of his bisexuality within the larger story arc is a needed reminder that hypermasculinity and biphobia do more than just oppress people who are on the receiving end of it; they develop spiritual death. I often found myself wanting to shake the author back to reality. The fundamental question the book wants us to answer: "where do we find love?" and its companion, "what do we do with it once we've found it?"

Lizet, Founder of Sexologybae.com a Black Millennial Perspective on Sex, Sexuality, and Relationships

"Victory's novella blows up the conventional narrative in order to explore culture, race, and, bisexuality. From Seoul to L.A. to São Paulo by way of New York, Ross Victory's genre-busting novella challenges all assumptions about race and sexuality. Complicated, and not at all conventional-- Victory presents us with no easy answers."

William E. Burleson, Author of Bi America – Myths, Truths, and Struggles of an Invisible Community

"Ross provides an enlightened view of sexuality that transcends the physical body. He shares his personal experiences with the struggles of being a Black bisexual male, dating across cultural lines personally and geographically, and the biases within the LGBT community toward bi-identifying people. Ross' voice is one that is gravely needed to normalize these experiences and push the newer generations into a more progressive future."

Jodie Shea, LMFT, Relationship, Sex & IFS Therapist
Pillow Talk Therapy

PANORAMA

THE MISSING CHAPTER FROM THE MEMOIR

VIEWS FROM THE COCKPIT: THE JOURNEY OF A SON

BY ROSS VICTORY

Created by J. Ross Victory
rossvictory.com
Cover illustration and interior illustrations by David Izaguirre, Jr.
izythereal.com
Cover graphic design and color by William Sikora III
sikoraentertainment.com
Interior layout by Vanessa Mendozzi
vanessamendozzidesign.com
Edited by Michael McConnel
Special thanks to all the beta readers for their feedback

ISBN 13: 9780578602158

www.rossvictory.com
viewsfromthecockpitbook@gmail.com

Panorama is a stand-alone, but related extension of *Views from the Cockpit: The Journey of a Son*. For the full narrative context and background of the events and characters in Panorama, the author strongly suggests reading the full memoir first.

Content Notice:

This book contains descriptive adult material (erotic scenarios and sharp language, and political rhetoric) that some audiences may find unsettling. The author recognizes the importance of providing this notice to readers.

DEDICATION

To the millions who build their house on a bridge deter-
mined not to light it on fire for shelter on the periphery.

'And besides all this, between us and you there is a great
chasm fixed, those who wish to come over from here to
you will not be able, and that none may cross over from
there to us.'

Luke 16:26

For J. Ross—a soul survivor

PANORAMA

Stand upright on top the highest mountains.

Grow your wings to glide between them.

Ascend. No matter the love. No matter the heartache.

Rise above short-lived stars,

Teleport between the holographic universe to chase the sun.

Awake. No matter the love. No matter the heartache.

Even then...

Even then—no matter how high I go,

No matter how infinite my east or vast my west

or how far I look back, behind and below,

Even at the altitude of atmospheric love

I can never reach or truly realize

The boundless beauty of the full Panorama.

Contents

DON'T BE A SISSY

"They're gonna give you a heart attack pill—nitroglycerin," my boss said.

"Nitro what?!" I could barely speak as my head tossed side to side. One of the Korean doctors grabbed my jaw. "Ib-eul yeol! Ib-eul yeol! Open!"

The doctor placed a nitroglycerin tablet under my tongue and quickly removed her hand from my mouth, which was beginning to tense, like lockjaw. A stern nurse tried to get me to stop flailing about long enough to plug me into a heart monitor. After several minutes, I finally ran out of energy to continue moving. My boss came over to my bed, her eyes watering with pity and sorrow, whispering to the Korean doctor looking down at me.

"Ross! They didn't find anything wrong with you," she

mumbled. "Breathe. Breathe, Ross. Breathe."

"What's going on with you?" She removed her glasses and wiped away a pooling tear in the corner of her eye. "Are you ok? You always seem so together," she said. "You should talk to someone..."

Somehow I hadn't noticed the overwhelming anxiety in my life until this point. I waited for someone to check in with me about my brother's brain cancer—hell, my dad's cancer, and the disbandment of my family. I kept waiting. Like a hitchhiker stuck in the vast Sahara Desert, imagining a car approaching in the distance as the flesh on his shoulders bled and scarred from the sun's blaze. Four words. That's all it would take to provide a layer of relief: *How. Do. You. Feel.* All of the physical sensations of anxiety felt normal to me. A skipping heartbeat felt normal. Shallow breathing felt normal. Sleepless nights felt normal until my body had enough.

Was the answer so simple? Just stop and breathe? That's it? My Seoul adventure had become a soul nightmare. My brother and his mysterious stage IV brain cancer had my family in a terror loop, as my dad frolicked around

China chasing vaginas, perched in emotional oblivion, my beloved mom rigid, inaccessible, in a corner, clutched to her Bible and pearls and me—once a boy with a fresh flat top, bugle sweater, and a picture-perfect smile, now seven thousand miles away from home with my foundation being ripped open, escaping the best I could, yet plugged into a machine in a society that couldn't care less about what I could or could not handle—if I died or lived, smiled or cried, coagulated or bled out. The exit route illuminated itself. It was time to take my ass home.

CROSS-CHECK

It was a freezing night in the peak of winter. Siberian winds moved down Russia and over the Korean peninsula, creating an excruciating, finger-numbing cold.

I found myself in a local bar called Panorama, skimming through my work contract. I contemplated my ability to continue this working abroad disaster and considered walking away from a large end-of-contract payment, or perhaps I was simply waiting for an explanation from "God" about why everything falls apart. I read the pages over and over, searching for what I needed to do to end my contract and still get the cash. Panorama was a quaint, local bar that Koreans escaped to to enjoy horrific karaoke and shots of throat-burning Soju, the equivalent of cheap vodka. Americans were not interested, nor did they notice this dingy place.

Tonight, it was fairly empty. Alone on the stage stood a Korean ahjumma, or aged woman. An ahjusshi, or aged man, also Korean, sat in flooded tan trousers on a short stool next to her, holding a large cello. The woman had a gray, shoulder-length poufy perm with a slight purple tint. She wore a hanbok—a traditional Korean dress—her face covered in thick, pasty-white makeup. With clarity, passion, and purpose, she and the cellist performed as no one but me watched. The song had a simple, memorable riff with a reflective chord progression. The woman had turned off the karaoke television screen and sang from memory as the cellist supported her.

She sang as if this were the last song she would ever sing. Her soul flickered between every note, with presence and awe. Like she was going somewhere and would never return. As the woman sang, she reached into the spotlight that lit her, pulling the light closer to her chest—like she and the light had established a deep state of devotion. As the ahjusshi played the cello, hidden in the woman's shadow, particles of dust floated through the light and disappeared into the darkness, like floating glowworms. I could not recognize her words but recognized the source of them. *This woman must be singing to me…* I thought. I fantasized about hope as she sang.

At one table, two Korean ahjummas laughed like schoolgirls, scrolling through their oversized smartphones. At another table, two businessmen had a drunken conversation about politics and kept saying "Obama" and "Romney" over and over. As I took inventory of the room, a group of four American soldiers entered Panorama. One soldier straggled behind the group. The door failed to fully close behind him, causing a glacial breeze to chill the air of the small bar. As I noticed the chill in the air, the woman finished her song. I clapped for her joyously.

Most of the military in Seoul were stationed in Itaewon, which was also the district for foreigners, or stationed in Uijeongbu, two hours away, protecting South Korea from North Korea. Large scale military drills across the city of Seoul were realities at the time to prepare for Kim Jong-Il's inevitable ire.

The four soldiers sat at the empty bar, near the stage. I

sat in an oversized, black leather booth near the entrance. One of the soldiers went back outside, propping the door open momentarily. The glacial breeze returned. The soldier strode back in and took a detour toward my booth, warming his hands. I turned away but could see him approaching from the corner of my eye.

"Ey, excuse me, bro. Restroom around here?" He shivered.

"Behind the bar…" I pointed.

After a few minutes, as I began to pack up, I heard a voice. "Ey, can I sit here? You look normal…" I looked up, confused. It was him again. He chuckled and shivered.

"Yeah, I'm headed out…all yours. Has a good view of the stage." I snickered to myself.

"Man, this woman can sing. I wonder what she's saying. I'm Alveré," the soldier continued, "Alvín in English. What you drinkin'?"

I motioned to my waiter for the check.

"Let me guess. You're from the West Coast," he said.

Alveré made it clear that he had time to chat and was looking for a friend. He removed his hat, placed it on the table, and rolled up his sleeves; he began flipping through the beer menu. Someone new in my life is the last thing I wanted.

Alveré had a slightly grown-in buzz cut and a naïve presence. He was dressed in army fatigues with coyote brown boots. He was covered in crisp snowflakes; Somehow, I could see the hexagonal and octagonal crystalline structure of the ice. His face was stuck in a half-smile, on the verge of a chuckle. He was nearly six feet tall with perfect posture and the typical, stiff, herculean stance of a military person.

He wore a forearm tattoo on his left arm of an Admiralty ship's anchor wrapped in chain links. The anchor transformed into a thirty-petal rose at the eye of the anchor. There was a hummingbird feeding on the rose, its wings curled in and up.

"Yep, from California—L.A. I'm Ross."

"Ross from Cali…" He seemed to contemplate this and quickly mumbled something in Portuguese. "Nice to meet you, Ross. I'm from New York, born in São Paulo, Brazil, though." "Moved here when I was thirteen." Alveré excitedly corrected himself, having momentarily forgotten that he was now in Korea. "You know what I mean…moved out *there*." He laughed.

"Brazil? How'd you get into the U.S. Army?"

"Long story. My unit just got here. I just met these idiots—FML." He continued. "You military? What are you doin' all the way in Korea…by yourself?"

"I'm actually an English teacher in a work-abroad program," I responded.

"You signed *up* to come here? Who does that?!"

I pondered, squinting my eyes. "I guess I did? What a dumbass." We laughed. "And I'm honestly sitting here regretting every moment." I held my contract up.

"Respect. Wow."

For the next several minutes, we spoke about the absurdities of Korean culture. Every time I glanced at Alveré to size him up, his eye contact felt like a Cyclops beam, at least for the fraction of a microsecond our pupils met. In these moments, the details of his eyes were apparent. His eyes were thalassic, deep, abidingly blue, with a thin chestnut lining. While intense and notably awkward, something about Alveré seemed familiar, like a puppy's gaze.

As we spoke, Alveré was wringing his hands on top of the table. He would rub his hands on the side of his pants and laugh randomly between longer gaps of silence, uttering, "Interesting!" at the end of my sentences. One of the other army guys tumbled into my booth.

"Hey, bro!" a drunken soldier said to Alveré.

"Ooh, he's sexy, Alvin! Did you get his number?" the solider drunkenly joked while reaching out and twisting Alveré's nipple. Alveré pulled away, embarrassed.

Another soldier interjected, "Alvin, you going tonight, bro? Rampant Korean pussy, bro…free flowing like *mas agua*." The soldier began to do the robot dance.

"Alvin's our new resident Brazilian model to attract that tiger pussy… Look at this face." The soldiers exploded into gut-wrenching laughter, grabbing Alveré's chin and squishing his lips. "Faggot," one soldier joked. "We're headed to this joint in Hungdae." Hungdae was Seoul's party capital. A night in Hungdae would mean we would be out until 6 a.m.

"You should join us…" The solider glanced over at

me. "I'm Connor." Connor reached out to shake my hand. He continued, "I hear they just let you…" The soldier paused, then wiggled his middle and ring finger around in quick circles. "And the girls just start makin' out with each other…They're all bisexual bro. All of 'em."

"You wanna roll through or…" The soldiers looked at me as Alveré hesitated. He whispered to me, "Don't leave me with these idiots. Please, bro, pleassssse!"

I explained to the soldiers that I was an English teacher and that my class started early. They became distracted and began to chatter drunkenly to each other.

"Please, Ross from Cali… Don't leave me with these douches—we vibin', right?"

I continued to pack my bag.

"I'll text you the address. Let me get your number. Just a few hours; never been to Hungdae…"

"Nice to meet you, Alveré, but I'm out..."

"My mom calls me Alveré; friends call me Alvin—you can call me Alví, though, if you want…" He continued. "You can tell me about L.A. I've always wanted to go there."

I laughed. I stared at my contract. My passport looked

back at me from the bottom of my bag. I looked back at Alví.

All right. I'm in, let's go.

AFTERBURN

For the next month, when everyone was dancing like drunk high schoolers on the top of bar tables until 6 a.m., then wobbling through the subway, belligerent and drunk, and I was rushing to teach Korean kids by 8 a.m., Alví became one of a handful of my friends in Korea who was interested in exploring Korea—its culture, its beauty, and all of its peculiarities. Alví was persistent and a king of follow-through, which made being flaky hard for me to accomplish.

Alví travelled by train for two hours into Seoul to meet up and do useless activities and have philosophical debates. His texts always began with: "Ross from Cali!" followed by something so lame that the level at which the lameness existed felt brilliant—almost captivating. Alví was someone who could sit and talk, club hop, and watch Korean game shows. He and I shared a love of music and Ford Mustangs.

Every week we discovered random parts of Seoul, exploring obscure places and getting into stupidity, which included haggling prices with old Korean ahjummas and mistakenly eating at dog cafés. Not cafés with newborn puppies running around in all their cuteness to keep guests entertained, but cafés that served actual chunks of dog meat, rabbit meat, and cat meat as part of their menu. The only way to find these places was from a native Korean or by accident.

We once visited a popular Korean restaurant that served San-nakji. San-nakji is a Korean dish of freshly detached octopus tentacles that wiggle around on a dinner plate. The octopus's death was so recent that nerve signals still flowed through the tentacles. The idea, supposedly, was to ingest pure energy from another, partially living being. I did not expect the tentacles to continue moving around after I began chewing them. As I began to chew a piece of San-nakji, a piece of tentacle crawled out of my mouth. Surprised by the tickle on my lip, I spit it out. It dove right into Alví's bean-paste soup, still squirming around for mercy or the ocean or someone to help it, making two grown men jump, knocking over our knee-high table and the twenty tiny plates of Korean side dishes, immediately infuriating several ahjusshis and ahjummas who looked on in hatred.

There was an air of ease and lightness that existed hanging out with Alví. As a introvert that could fake extroversion, I had never been able to spend hours with people without finding at least two things annoying about their personality, gestures or voice rhythm or wondering how and when they would try to rob or stab me. Alví couldn't be boxed in—he was stiff *and* clumsy. A rebel *and* conservative. Smart yet naïve. As an afro-Brazilian, Alví enjoyed dancing rumba and hip hop, yet he could load an automatic rifle within seconds in a state of complete chaos. Something about him felt like me, but freer and more trusting. He was buoyant and free yet able to portray instant depth. I respected the range of his personality.

The drama in my life felt like it lost its sting as this friendship came to fruition. Time began to pass quickly. The anxiety that had built up about my brother's cancer, which had triggered a hypochondriacal response in me and the need to get *my* brain scanned, the death of my family unit, and the overall frustration of living in Korea seemed to numb, or maybe it was the Xanax. Although my dad and Vee lived right across the Yellow Sea in China at the time, things felt less craptacular and were digestible now that I had someone to make fun of them with and someone who could truly understand the level of absurdity.

Over time, Alví finally told me that he was not a citizen of the United States despite having a perfect California-sounding accent. He moved to the U.S. as a teenager and learned English from watching the TV show *Friends*. Alví had received his green card and the next step was to serve honorably in the U.S. military for at least one year to be eligible for naturalization, which would then make him eligible for permanent citizenship. Serving in South Korea was something he had to do or else somehow marry an American.

We continued to share more about our backgrounds— the good, the bad, and the deeply personal. Alví revealed how his parents had fled Rio De Janeiro to the U.S. to escape a group of Brazilian gangsters. They had lived a luxurious life from the millions his father had made as a drug dealer until they lost everything in a drug bust, requiring his father to pay off the police and local politicians but indebted to a violent drug lord. Over time, his parents had grown to despise each other for the dysfunction of their new American life. His father worked as a mechanic barely able to speak English, and his mother worked as a maid. They insisted on staying together in order to prevent abandoning Alví and his siblings in a new country. Alví described how his father would transform into an abusive alcoholic, and how he had fist-fought him several times to protect his mother and sisters. "There's nothing like hitting the old man for the first time," he said. "I felt like I had to... he fucked up our whole life. I can only dream that he would escape with some random Chinese hoe," he continued.

Although Alví had great affinity for America, he was relieved to escape his family through the military. He explained how his ex-girlfriend and high school sweetheart, Nerissa, was the only one who knew about his legal issues and his family's entrenchment with Brazilian gangsters. And now, me. The U.S. military was the epitome of safety.

Spring was quickly approaching. Mild breezes, Mandarin sunsets, and the silhouettes of ancient South Korean temples began to slowly defrost winter. By this point, I had mastered ordering Korean food for delivery. This particular night, we ordered traditional marinated Korean bulgogi beef and white rice. After hours of trying to make sense of Korean gameshows and ranting about the people back in our home lives, we began to talk about relationships and dating.

We joked about the absurdities of dating in Seoul, and how no one in Korea seemed to have any ass. No bounce. No filled jeans, nothing to ease the libido of a black and Brazilian men, whose cultures' both stereotypically prioritized the occurrence of sensuous, syrupy, soap-soaked buttocks, and the ability to look at the world through "ass glasses."

"So…these Koreans eating you up, huh? I'm sure you got all kinds of people on speed-dial," Alví said shyly.

"Nah, just my co-worker Sasha," I laughed. "But Sasha….she's busy captivating the hearts and bodies of her innocent Korean co-teachers… one of Sasha's co-teachers wears homemade plaid dresses and brings her lunch in a Hello Kitty plastic lunchbox."

I continued. "Sasha turns these girls out, hangs 'em to dry, ghosts them, and they become suicidal. It's a bit tragic, but hilarious to watch. She's on her fourth co-teacher." We exploded in laugher. Alví uttered something in Portuguese.

"Yea, some days I don't know who to expect, but she's cool people, though; super metaphysical, super bisexual," I continued. "Her presence is in her eyes, so mysterious. Oh and heart-shaped areolas—I swear…"

"Interesting," Alví nodded.

We expanded our conversation about Sasha's sexual fluidity into contemplation if God was a man or a woman or had mostly male or female essence.

"C'mon, Ross, we can never know the answer to that." Alví laughed. "Are you trying to justify you and Sasha??"

We began to debate if assigning a male role to the essence of God contributed to the oppression of women in societies by requiring their reliance on God, and thereby men, in failed social systems. There's not many people willing to discuss that for fun.

"Yo! Leave it for the philosophers…"

Alví pressed down on the building tension in my right

shoulder with his fingers.

I continued, excited. "But if we (humans) are products of God, then God, the creator, must be the indisputable source of men and women—right?"

The source of masculinity—strength in shoulders. The source of femininity—strength in heart. Men and women put us in touch with God, the creator.

Alví began to knead my shoulders and trapezius with his knuckles.

"Look at all this stress you're causing yourself," he snickered. "Who cares?"

"Do you think some of us are born emptier in one source or the other, though? What if you're empty in both?" Fascinated by this concept that I had uncovered, I continued to ramble without a response. Alví interrupted.

"So you're saying you think I'm God, Ross?" Alví got closer to me, massaging my tense neck more intensely.

"Probably…" We paused. I could hear the synchronized ticks of the wall clock, crisper than ever. At least fifteen seconds elapsed. Alví uttered something in Portuguese.

"You're always sayin' shit in Portuguese… What are

you saying?!"

"Me da um beijo."

"Huh?" I attempted to repeat the phrase. *"Me da um bey*-what?"

"Okay, Ross, I didn't realize you felt that way."Alví chuckled and leaned in toward me. "That means 'kiss me' in Portuguese. You said it…"

I leaned back. "Finally!" The sound of the ticking wall clock returned for another five seconds. "How do you say it again?"

"Me da um beijo."

"Ok."

What happened next runs the risk of being shockingly traumatic. Tempted to change your life through a defiant description, I'll go with: adrenaline popped through my skin like a wave of tiny firecrackers.Within seconds, I felt like I had kissed the sun—purposely, finally, and appropriately. I could feel thousands of small hairs on my neck raise one by one, even the hairs in my ear like the energy produced by millions watching the Superbowl, painstakingly, for hours. Down by three with thirty seconds left and from sheer luck, an Onside-Kick returns to the losing team and the star quarterback sprints to secure the most shocking win in NFL history. The cheers—the deep rumble of the crowd—explode in hysteria and approval and relief. I laughed to myself. *Are all the foreigners here bisexual?*

Over time, some days I caught myself thinking about Alví while he sat right in front of me. *How can you miss someone who is right in front of you?* In the corner of my mind, I felt troubled—not from crossing a physical line or discovering anything new about my sexual capacity, but from Alví's specific afterburn. Emotional detachment was a skill I had developed in a competitive dating space, but something about Alvi's "after flame" did not scorch, but soothed. I had only felt like this level of intensity one other time, as a teenager and with a woman. The feeling is frightful to a callous heart. In the past, it had caused years of obsession and willingness to blow up my life. It feels like everything else means nothing. To know that, in fact, there are people roaming around who have the ability to pull back layers and to know that this level of intensity is available for me to experience in this life felt like magic. Whenever we went somewhere, we might as well have been bobble-heads skipping through daisy fields in sheer joyous ridiculousness.

To entertain ourselves, Alví decided that we should prepare a backstory and conjure up how we'd met each other, as our friend networks began to overlap. Soldiers and contract teachers typically did not frequent the same places or have a reason to know each other. Alví decided that it made the most sense to say, "We're friends from the States." All the foreigners in Korea talk and gossip to each other about other foreigners. Alví's plan worked well until my co-worker Sasha followed up with a simple question. Alví fumbled into awkward laughter and graceless groans. Her question? *"Which state?"* As Alví spoke, Sasha squinted her eyes in suspicion, listening to Alví's choppy explanation and nodding and batting her eyes with a phony smile. She looked over at me coquettishly, nodding her head in playful skepticism, finally rolling her eyes.

Sasha was five feet two inches tall, curvy, but more athletic. She was biracial (half black, half Korean), working abroad on an extended work contract. Sasha's skin was a medley of cream, vanilla and dark roast coffee—a shade of butterscotch, with Asian spiced freckles. She was experimental with her hair. She alternated between a mohawk braid topknot; half cornrows, half straight; spring twists with blonde highlights and her natural waist length bouncy curls. She was born in South Korea but had moved to Oregon with her parents at five years old, never learning the Korean language. She moved back to Seoul to escape her parents, who had begun to hoard cats, and to pursue her dream of becoming a professional backup dancer for K-Pop stars. She lived with her Korean grandparents and taught English to support herself financially.

Although Sasha was an accomplished dancer in America and had danced on some of the biggest stages in the world, Koreans did not feel that she was Korean enough, by blood or background, to participate in their culture, not to mention dance among major K-Pop stars. All the while it was Sasha's racial ambiguity, her status as *biracial*, that bode well for her on the American dance scene. Sasha often expressed deep stress from not being black enough or Korean enough to thrive in both worlds. She embraced her background but felt people constantly pressuring her to pick a side in all senses of herself—pick a race, pick a culture, pick men or women, pick fried chicken or kimchi. The social issues between blacks and Koreans that originated during the L.A. riots made her feel uncomfortable at family gatherings growing up. Sasha's black and Korean family were relentless in their expressions of hate for each other, often forgetting Sasha had one black and one Korean parent. It wasn't until Sasha's Korean grandmother told Sasha, as an adult, that it was ok for her to be black, that she began to feel safe in her mixed background. Sasha and I had become friends and bored lovers after I found astrology books and books from the philosopher Osho on her work desk. She was neat, forward and assertive. She always smelled like sparkly citrus. After Alví botched our storyline, Sasha looked at me and bit her bottom lip with thoughtful seduction.

"Ross is in these streets…" she laughed, checking out Alví, packing up her up items.

"I would love to hear more about this, but I gotta run. Toodles." Sasha tossed her hair back and began to wrap her long kinky curls into the ease of a bun. She covered her hair with headscarf, her heels clacking down the hallway.

With a coy smile, she looked back at us waving.

"Yo! What was that?" I asked Alví.

"Her eyes made me nervous..."

"'Cause she's not stupid. From now on, you draw up the plans and let me talk," I laughed.

During this period, my dad and I lived in the same time zone. As a new retiree, he lived on and off in Eastern China and his friend's cold garage. My dad enjoyed health, mobility, and was recently divorced from my mom. He lived with Vee and worked part-time teaching Chinese kids English. Speaking to him even momentarily enraged me. Everything about him seemed like a phony used-car salesman trapped in a double life.

"Are you gonna tell Pops and his crazy Chinese lady about me?" Alví asked innocently as he swiped and scrolled through his phone. "Nerissa's texting me again! She wants to get married!" he uttered in annoyance.

"Tell him what about you? Are you gonna tell your ass-beating father about *me*?"

"Whoa there…touchy are we? He wouldn't mind about us; all he thinks about is the Brazilian mafia," he laughed.

Triggered, I explained to Alví that as a teenager when my desires became more apparent and undeniable, I rather jump from a thirty-story roof full speed into the pavement with a packed audience of familiar faces pleading me to step back than to attempt to explain (and justify) anything sexual to my familial network.

"I once found a forty-page plus report in my dad's writings about why he felt same-sex relationships were sinful…I think I was thirteen when I found that. Funny, right?" Even more traumatic was the realization of the opposite-sex feelings that also did not go away.

The choices were, in fact, football games or drag shows, both entertaining, but none of which evoke the slightest excitement to return in me. Labels felt disingenuous because no-one could really capture all of my interests; growing up, authenticity felt impossible. As I was at eleven years old, taught to refrain from expressing or challenging my understanding of the world to the queen of knowledge—my grandma, matriarch of Tiffany Church—was still felt true. Refrain. Don't make waves. Don't you *ever* say, think or do something outside of what you've been shown.

"That doesn't sound easy. Live yo!" Alví reassured.

My cell phone rang and, ironically, it was my dad and Vee, who had called to wish me happy birthday. I sat, disgusted, listening, as my dad passed the phone to Vee.

"Alví, you know what…you're right… maybe I should tell him about you—to retaliate as a punch line to this joke of a family. Everyone gets to do what they want so I should be afforded that opportunity. "*Ey dad, whoo-hoo you out here f*cking these Chinese hoes from the church congregation, and I'm out here f*cking soldiers. SOLDIERS and bisexual hoes*—I see you, Pops, let's get it in. High five!"

"Damn…you think of me as retaliation…" Alví asked disappointedly. "It sounds like he really respects you…If my dad fell over from a heart attack right now, I'd celebrate," he continued.

We continued for several minutes. Alví said that his family went to mass, but never took Catholicism seriously. He was more troubled by how Brazilian men overstate their manhood to try to attract women. Ultimately to mistreat them and neglect multiple, separate, minivans full of their kids. Alví told me that he had never been able to recover from the guilt of hitting his father. He felt justified to protect his mom. Still, on the other hand, he contemplated what type of person could hit a parent.

"We gotta be better, Ross…" Alví insisted.

The next week, I decided to visit China for my dad's birthday and returned to Seoul within a week. I discovered that there was another woman who kept my dad coming to China. *You ever wonder why your dad keeps coming to China?* one of his friends said. *Her.* My dad heard his friend make this comment. He scolded him in the corner of a restaurant as I sat next to this woman. *Why could I never muster up the courage to confront my dad about what I felt to be hypocrisy?* The woman he was referring to and who sat next to me was not Vee, but the woman we had met on our very first trip to China long before the divorce. The woman from the blind children's hospital. I could not take any more of these fake, lying, false prophets!

YOU GOOD?

Several more months flew by. It was now the end of summer. Alví, Sasha, and I had been club hopping and drinking for several hours with some teachers before we found ourselves in a Jamaican-themed nightclub. The three of us shared a table, fresh pineapple and apple slices, and shots of Patron. It was nearly 3 a.m., and our group began to disband.

The DJ mixed up the song, and the crowd exploded in approval as the bassy, syncopated Afrobeat track was layered with a heavy synth and soft snaps mixed in. The bass dropped again. Sasha pulled me onto the dance floor, almost spilling my OJ and vodka cocktail on her cream-colored pantsuit.

Sasha began to slow wind down my leg to the bass of the music as the beat settled in. She removed her zebra print high heels and quickly applied lip gloss and checked her reflection in a tiny makeup mirror. She tossed her hair in slow motion—the blue and green neon lights shot through strands of her hair and the darkness perfectly accenting her pose. Her eyes sparkled in slow motion like fireworks on the Fourth of July. She tossed her curls across my face. Her hair left traces of vanilla and coconut on me. I closed my eyes as she slow-grinded in circles up and down my leg, gazing up at me in virginal innocence. Sasha put her arms around my neck and wrapped her left leg around my waist. Alví sat at the bar sipping his beer with a slightly bewildered frown, confused, watching us dance.

Sasha over me? Fa real... he mouthed, then shrugged and looked down at his phone. He waved his phone at me. "Guess who's texting again?"

Sasha leaned back, her leg and my back supporting her.

"Come here…" She motioned with her finger to Alví as we swayed in unison.

Alví fumbled and spit out his beer.

Almost without hesitation Alví began to dance over

to us—parting water and Harlem Shaking.

"Alví, nobody is Harlem Shakin' in 2011…"

Sasha turned around, pressing her butt in my crotch, leaning back so her neck met my chin, cuing me to kiss her. I moved my tongue in tiny wet circles and soft flicks and sucks on her warm neck. She panted in pleasure. She continued to sway her body in pulsating circles—alternating between a staccato twerk and a quick two-step, all in perfect sync with the thump of the percussion in the Afrobeat song. Alví looked alarmed.

"Don't shame me, Alví…"

"I didn't say anything!" Alví gushed.

"Your eyes…are you scared of a woman that knows what she wants?" Sasha asked. "Do I make you uncomfortable?"

Sasha wrapped her right hand around my head and grabbed Alví's butt cheeks. She quickly bounced it with her fingers before clinching his cheek tightly to bring him closer.

The club had gathered around us, cheering us on. I could see Sasha's frumpy Korean co-teacher across the dance floor, sitting alone, saddened, with a notebook.

Koreans watched us in amazement, gawking and staring at Alví and Sasha's dancing ability. Surely, it was not me, trying to keep up with them. A chubby drunk Korean woman with inch-thick eyeglasses and shiny round cheeks jumped on a table and took out her wallet and started fanning Korean won, Korean money. The music or something had overtaken us because I didn't know where Sasha ended and Alví began, or maybe it was the Patrón.

Sasha took my right hand and began to move it down the inside of her pantsuit, over her clammy, glittery breasts and erect nipples, down her torso and onto the top of her waist. "You remember how I like it, Ross?" she whispered biting my earlobe. She was not wearing panties. Alví came closer and began to slow wind down Sasha. She put her hand on top of his head moving her fingers through his loose curls while guiding my hand closer to her inner thighs.

Sasha whispered and giggled, "Devil's triangle, gentlemen?" Alví danced back up. Sasha surprisingly turned around and aggressively pressed her buttocks into Alví's crotch, quickly dipping low and grabbing her ankles.

I hollered in laughter from the shocking move. They both stopped dancing. "Yeah, you're invited all right," I said before the fat Korean woman called out to us in anger to continue dancing, interrupting me. Alví began to laugh-cough.

Coughing repeatedly, he croaked, "Be right back." He began to gag and hold his breath. Alví took off toward the restroom.

Thirty minutes had gone by, and Alví had not returned. Sasha and I waited at our booth discussing her invite and her plans for us.

"Sasha, you are too much…"

"You may wanna check on bae," she said sarcastically.

I went into the club's restroom. I found Alví passed out and spread out on the bathroom floor under a stall in his vomit, moaning in discomfort. Three young Korean men were rummaging through his jacket for his wallet and cell phone.

"American," one of the men uttered to the others flipping through Alví's passport and wallet.

"Ey!" I shouted, startling the group. *"Jae-ki-ral!?"* I yelled in Korean, which means *What the f*ck!?*

"Get the f*ck off of him!" I pulled the Korean men away from Alví. One man reached for Alví's wallet. I jabbed him sharply in his face with my elbow, causing blood to eject from his nose. He lost balance.

"Dowajo! Dowajo!" I yelled. "Help!"

One of the Korean men hopped on my back. His friend tripped me and we fell to the floor, swishing through blood and Alví's baby-food-colored vomit. The Korean man wrapped his arms around my neck in a headlock; I kicked, squirming for air. Alví rolled from under the stall and kicked the man's chin, releasing his headlock on me. I got on top of the man and began to punch him repeatedly. Alví tripped and kicked the man's friends as they tried to stop me. I began to black out, barely able to discern my fist bashing the man's face into the brown-stained toilet rim. I could see his soul in his eyes, pleading me to stop.

I broke the toilet paper holder and began to jab his face with the edge of the holder. We swished through pee, blood, and vomit as I tried to keep my position steady over his face. One of his teeth fell out and blood began to gush from his mouth. I used my knuckles and dug into his eyes sharply. The man hollered as I asked him repeatedly *You wanna take something?*

"Ross, STOP!!" Alví shouted.

I began to jab and twist the toilet holder into the man's ear.

"ROSS!! LEAVE HIM, I'M OK! LOOK—I'M OK." Alví hollered.

Distracted by Alví's wail, the Korean man's friends pulled me back. I lunged toward the man again, who was whining in pain covering his face. I spit in his face, gasping like a beast. The friends collected each other and scrambled out of the small bathroom. I threw a soap container at them as the door closed.

I paced the bathroom in fury and sweat. "Alví, you good? You drink too much? F*ck those guys." I was so angry and numb that I had not noticed a huge piece of skin dangling from my elbow. All the buttons on my shirt had been broken.

Alví shivered on the bathroom tile. "Give me a sec, just a bit sick," he uttered.

I propped open the bathroom door. I could see Sasha

across the club. I motioned for her to come over to the restroom. She gestured back: *one minute*. I motioned for Sasha's Korean co-teacher to get Sasha.

"Ross from Cali…" Alví mumbled, reaching for my pant leg.

"Hold up. Sasha is comin' to help…" A few minutes passed.

"Where is this damn girl?" Frantically, I ran searching for Sasha through the crowd of drunken clubgoers. The club was overtaken by strobe lights and thumping bass, making Sasha impossible to locate. People began to come into the bathroom, throwing up and pissing on the floor around us. Alví asked repeatedly to lie down. I called Sasha, but her phone had been switched off, so we took off toward the club exit, hailing a taxi to my apartment.

For the next thirty minutes, I watched as Alví retched into a plastic bag in the back of a taxi—still confident that he would be okay. I asked Alví to walk me through everything he had eaten throughout the day and all of his allergies.

"I'm good, I'm good. I just need to lie down for a bit."

"Yo! If you die…"

We finally arrived at my apartment. I called the

International Helpline for emergency assistance in English. I explained how Alví could not hold down water and randomly made violent jerking eye movements. I could not fully understand the nurse's accent, but finally she advised me to hang up the phone and to call the ambulance immediately. Alví refused. He argued that without a native Korean translator, anything could happen to him in an ambulance and ER room. He assured me he just needed to lie down.

"Are you sure??" I asked.

For several hours, Alví lay across my bathroom floor, drenched in sweat, alternating between shivering and uncontrollable flatulence. While Alví slept between attacks, I called his ex-girlfriend Nerissa with the idea that she would know what to do or what was happening. Nerissa was the last person Alví had texted. Surprisingly, she knew who I was and greeted me warmly on the phone. I explained Alví's condition. Nervously, Nerissa explained Alví's Meniere's disease, an inner ear disorder that caused vertigo attacks and dizzy spells triggered by stress from migraines. Alví refused the ER again, unaware that I was on his phone.

Nerissa offered to guide me through the relief steps she had learned during one of Alví's attacks in high school. She told me to lay him across a table, positioning his neck over the side. For the next thirty minutes, Nerissa walked me through the steps to stop Alví's sensation of spinning and dizziness.

"Who's on the phone?" Alví mumbled repeatedly as we went through the steps to regain his balance. "Don't call Nerissa…" he whispered, as I moved his head around in circles. Nerissa heard his comment and asked me for clarification of what Alví had said, which I ignored.

Slowly Alví became lucid. After another hour, Alví was able to sit up and finally able to walk. We rode the subway for the next few hours back to the military base in Uijeongbu, stopping every fifteen minutes for him to throw up in the subway restrooms. We finally made it back to Uijeongbu, where the military doctors hooked him up to IVs and treated him for a severe vertigo attack.

Within weeks, Nerissa spontaneously flew to Seoul to visit Alví. During her visit, I did not hear from Alví much. I had anticipated meeting Nerissa and thanking her for her help, but we never met, due to schedule conflicts and distance.

After Nerissa left, Alví and I met up at a famous French restaurant that overlooked Seoul. Modern Korean art paintings and ivory sculptures covered the walls. A huge three-story glass wall overlooked a lush garden crowded with red Korean pine and yellow Gingko trees. The garden was surrounded by Korean temples, with a large five-story pagoda in the center. In the opposite direction of the garden, there were miles and miles of city lights. The panorama was stunning. I told Alví that I was going to return home. My contract was finally nearing completion, and I needed to go home to try to face the issues that were waiting for me. Alví asked me over and over to stay until his service ended so that we could go back to the U.S. together. I couldn't take one more moment in Seoul. We agreed to meet up in L.A. and designed a grand scheme on how to sustain *us* back home. It only made sense that we escape dysfunction together. I returned to L.A. and Alví returned to New York six months later. We had promised to stay in touch no matter what life threw at us. We kept in contact, communicating often by text or Skype.

When I returned to L.A., I moved back into my mom's home and quickly got a job as an English teacher at a community college. I did not realize how much internal growth had occurred during my time in South Korea and was yet to understand the depth of the growth. Everything that I had sought to escape waited patiently for my return. My mom began to have chest pains as my dad amped up the pressure of the divorce and took claim of half of her retirement. My brother continued to have brain surgeries to remove the cancer. My dad lived on and off in China. I sulked in the reality, which was full of sadness and monotony. South Korea; Alví; Sasha; my friends; the clubbing; dog cafes; octopus tentacles; neon lights. It all felt like a lucid hallucination. For years, I would dream of walking down Seoul's streets and the smell of Tteok-bokki or stir-fried rice cakes. I could still smell Korean BBQ wafting in my apartment window and the rhythm of subway doors opening and closing. I could still see the glare and snarl of the old Korean ahjummas and ahjusshis, which now felt humorous and much easier to forgive. *Was it just a dream?*

CONSIDERATIONS

After an exhausting day of teaching adults English at a local community college, I received an e-mail from Nerissa. Over the years, we typically did not communicate aside from the surface-level "happy birthday" or "Merry Christmas" messages on Facebook or Skype. E-mailing back and forth was surely not something we did. The email's subject line was "Considerations."

The e-mail started off endearing, articulating how impressed she was with my Facebook persona of travel adventurer. Quickly, though, Nerissa informed me that she and Alví were expecting a child—a son. I was shocked. Mostly because it was Nerissa informing me. Nerissa expressed inescapable joy that God would trust her to carry a child and unshakeable gratitude that the father was Alví.

Halfway through the e-mail, Nerissa began to express anxiety at the thought of becoming a single mom. She said that she didn't know if it was her hormones or her mind, but the panic felt debilitating as the child grew inside her and as she contemplated her son's future. Nerissa wrote that she *"envisioned losing Alvin and pictured him with someone less dramatic, less pregnant and more polished than me or being killed by someone searching for his family."* Throughout the e-mail, Nerissa said that she didn't know what her e-mail's purpose was and just two hours ago hadn't anticipated sending the e-mail.

The tone changed and began to feel manipulative. Toward the end of the message, Nerissa began to ask for my support. Nerissa told me that she empathized with me and Alví, stating that she knew that there are many isolating moments for "men like us." She said that she understood the value of finding someone who gets it. *"It's definitely one-sided,"* she wrote. *"Honestly, I don't envision a place in society for masculine bi-men—at least the ones who are truly impassioned from physical and emotional access to men and women—our culture will never get it."*

She said that Alví had been distancing himself because he feels left out of the process of the pregnancy. *"I cannot do it alone and I need him more than ever and I don't know if I should be sharing him. I hope you understand me, Ross."* I wondered what she meant by share. Nerissa explained how she was the product of a broken home and how her father had walked out on her mom, two sisters, and little brother, who were all under the age of ten at the time. He started a new family with her mom's childhood best friend and erased them out of his memory, becoming unreachable and moving out of the country. Nerissa explained how her resentment of her father followed her and affected every male relationship in her life except the one with Alví. *"He's one of the only men I don't resent. That means something."*

She continued *"Ross, I wonder, do you care enough to let Alvin be the full-time father I need him to be right now?"* She went on to describe how she had heard about my dad and what happened with the crazy Chinese lady and how debilitating his actions had been, causing me to move to Korea in a fit of anger. *"Great men like you and like Alvin are hard to find. Please don't misunderstand me, but Alvin is all I have—he will be all this child has."*

Nerissa ended the letter with: *"I'm bringing this to you in confidence."*

After I read the letter, I closed my laptop to sit and think. I sat staring at the wall, processing what had just happened and wishing I had someone to call for advice. This felt like one of those high school breakups where your girlfriend's (or boyfriend's) friend tells you are scheduled to break up.

Immediately, I leaned into my privilege. I told myself that I did not care about Alví or Nerissa. They were both lunatics and I could simply forget and choose not to share their existence. I felt overwhelming anger as the pieces and details settled into place. Did Nerissa just conquer and divide to engulf someone who actually understood me? I hollered at the wall, throwing my laptop across the room shattering it into pieces.

Like a sorcerer from Dungeons and Dragons, Nerissa

crafted words, which could not be unread or mistaken, to summon absolute distortion.

WI-FI IN THE SKY

Alví and I began to contact each other less and less. It had been several months, and neither of us had the money to facilitate the meeting we had planned in Seoul. As time passed, the shock settled in from Nerissa's letter. It was approaching two years since I'd returned to L.A. from Seoul—and nearly one year since we had seen each other in person. Nearly a month had passed since I'd received Nerissa's message, and Alví never mentioned that Nerissa was pregnant. A few weeks had gone by since we last spoke. I had returned from a working summer in Miami.

First message from Alví mentioning the pregnancy

Alví: Ross from Cali, talk to me! I need to hear about Miami asap………So, I'm gonna be a father!!!!! Nerissa's preggo. I tried to call, but let's Skype if you're around… maybe tomorrow? I'll be done at 4.

Two days later

Alví: Ross from Cali, where you been bro? Pick up your Skype!! How's your dad and bro doin? He still with that crazy Chinese lady?

A week later

Alví: Ey man, just thought about that night at the Jamaican club…Lmao!! Ross from Cali saved Alveré from Brasil. Dats love yo. You still talk to Sasha? She was down. My bad for getting sick. Haha. You must be busy af. Text me.

Next day

Alví: Wyd? I see you been reading the messages. You good??

I had begun to distract myself with work and online dating, which was growing in popularity, to avoid having the need to reach out to Alví and respond. In fact, I wanted to talk, but I restrained myself. I didn't know what to say or how to civilly bring up the message Nerissa had sent me. I was unsure of what I wanted to say, stuck between feelings of rejection and the desire to forgive. I prepared to move out of my mom's house and into the dingy, shared home of an eighty-year-old Finnish woman, which was a book worthy experience itself. Around the same time, my family began to understand that the death of my brother was near. I had yet to unpack a lifetime of unlabeled resentment, and this prevented me from being able to communicate and understand where I found myself. That is to say, Nerissa's wishes that I disappear from their life began to manifest naturally.

E-mail the next day

Alví: Did I say something wrong? Sup w/ u

A week later

Alví: Ross, I'm sure you see me blowin up your phone. Nerissa told me about that psycho ass e-mail she sent you!!!!!!! That was so fucked up!!! I didn't talk to her for a week…. I couldn't believe she'd do that shit. Don't over-think it, we're good. I just wanted to make sure nothing happened with the pregnancy. My sister had four miscarriages and you can jinx them. I swear. If you tell people too soon, it can be bad if it doesn't work out… Me not tellin you doesn't mean I didn't want you to know. Please contact me.

Same day, hours later

Nerissa doesn't know what she's talking about. U know she's just pregnant and needs that extra D and attention, right? Everything irritates her and smells bad. She makes me wear a helmet in the car! It's rough, but she's carrying my son, so what should I do??? Can we talk though?? I need to ask you something... You know you're gonna be the godfather right? A godfather with benefits ;)
I see you and pops in Costa Rica? How's he? You stay travelin'. WHO ARE YOU? :)

Two weeks later.

Alví: ………How was Costa Rica? Worried…a month,

no talk? No text? No e-mail? Am I being ghosted?

Every person I attempted to "date," every time I went out, I felt deeply unfulfilled and uninterested. Interactions with people lacked depth. I found myself rating people on a simple scale...not of f*ckability, but on their ability to help me through a spell of vomiting or my willingness to whoop someone's ass to protect them. I could only wonder if they were worth the effort. Most felt like empty bags of flesh. I began to wonder what would happen if I never responded to Alví again. He would eventually have to stop. Unfriending him on social media seemed like an appropriate first step.

A week later

Alví: Hey Ross, this is Nerissa. Can you respond to Alvin? Sorry about my e-mail. I wanna speak to you about it... Too pregnant to think straight.

Four days later

Alví: WTF! Unfriended? What did I do?? You haven't

said anything in over a month. Is that a mistake?

Next day

    Alví: Unfriended...smh.

Two days

    Alví: Wow, I was unfriended for real...

An hour later

    Alví: U know what, U really don't know how much it took for me to talk to you that night in Seoul....I could never tell you the panic I felt. You are the first man that I approached in public—I practiced in the bathroom like an idiot...

Minutes later

That means something to me, does that mean anything to you???? Do you even know what it's like to take a risk like that? No b/c you're made of fear.

A few hours later

Nerissa said she is sorry about the letter… Of course, I was going to tell you. YOU KNOW that, too. F*ck, what is up with you??? Are you ok?

You can't even tell me what's going on, yet you want me to see that you're reading my messages. I need to hear from you asap!! I'm getting pissed.

[attaches photos from Seoul]

????

A few hours later

Alví: Your words: "Is God a man or a woman?" Do you remember that conversation, or have you unfriended that out of your memory too? Remember, you said you had never met someone like me and that we were the same person…I felt that. You just say that to everyone?! Americans are so fake.

A few hours later

I don't know why I keep trying to call you, lol. If you don't want to be my Facebook friend, that's fine, but I know what happened in real life…You can't just disappear on people when you feel vulnerable, Ross. Isn't that what your family has done…run away and sweep things under the rug with no conversation or effort? I am so sorry that Nerissa sent that stupid ass message!!! I'm tryin to figure this out. Idk what to do. I'm trying to call u, we can't just text this. You're my boy, she's my girl—period. Don't X me out Ross... Remember what we planned….

An hour later

Ya know what, f*ck it. Me and Nerissa are gonna get married... I wanted to tell you first…bc you're literally one of my best friends… I think everything will be easier with my citizenship if we're married.

Ross: I never disputed what happened in "real life." WTF are you talking about??

I did feel Seoul *was* a dream, but as more and more time went on, I began to feel more had taken place below the surface with Alví than I anticipated, and now I was over three thousand miles away trying to understand all of this against everything else that was already spiraling. Looking back, only Alví understood the stakes.

Next day

Alví: You don't think Korea was real—I understand who you are. You don't have a fucking clue what's real. Lol. You're making me a victim of your suspicion... DON'T F*CKING RESPOND. Just remember it was me who was there when you had nowhere to go and no one to talk to, popping your anxiety pills. But I know guys like u. We call this *Garotinha*, little dickless boy. You push away the person who actually cares about you. Hahahah!

Ross: Your "real" vomit was on me. I carried your real limp body up and down the subway stairs…I fought people off of you and now I have a scar on my arm. I don't know what's real?? I don't speak. I act. You can write whatever you want, call me names… but my behavior speaks for itself…and what exactly have you done for me but add drama and pain to my life?

I don't have to prove anything to you…you should know how I feel. Should I have left your ass in that stall and ran off to f*ck Sasha while you got robbed and died DUMMY. YOU do not have a clue. Lmao!!!!!!! Btw, you aren't brave for talking to strangers in bars. You're entitled. You're careless.

Minutes later

If you wanna say shit to me, say it in English. Stop hidin behind language – *GAROTINHA.*

Hour later

Alví: I'll delete you out of my memory, then. You're the one who said I come up with the ideas and you execute??????? LOOK WHAT YOU'RE DOING. I'VE SENT YOU MESSAGE AFTER MESSAGE - NO RESPONSE, TOLD YOU SORRY ABOUT THAT E-MAIL, I CHECK ON YOU ALL THE TIME, AND YOU SAY I DON'T VALUE? Looks like you're on a road to being a selfish ass prick just like your dad! World WATCH OUT. If the father is any indication, then we're screwed!! There will be a mountain of corpses from the people you hurt, starting with me. Go ahead and write a song about it. No one will listen anyway.

Ross: I'm glad I finally know that you are cold and disgusting. Esp since Nerissa referenced my dad in her message... Why would she know anything about him and what he's doing in China and how I feel about my family!?!?! She could only know that.......through u. AND THEN SHE USED THAT TO ACCOMPLISH WHATEVER IS IN HER MIND...me being selfish? You didn't notice that major detail because.......you're entitled.

Cell phone rings

I don't wanna talk to you...just take responsibility for Nerissa. Whatever she is...she's actin like a narcissistic b*tch, for real. Do u even know her??? Because of *your* error and *your* fumble all of this is occurring. All u. Wake up.

Minutes later

You never introduced me to Nerissa, never put us in the same room or got us on the phone to plan this out and set some kind of boundaries about how this shit is supposed to go—why is that??? And then you bring ME into your hot mess of a life…I do everything I can to be a good person to you…. you don't care to see it. So yeah, YOU don't value this enough to take proper care of people you claim you care so much about. Men keep their house in order – don't know wtf this is…

Cell phone rings

Cell phone rings two hundred and seventy times over the next ten hours

One month later

Alví: Ross, this is Nerissa. Can you call us, please? Alví had another attack. This was a bad one. He fell and got a concussion. We've been in ICU for two days and he wants to talk to us. I think I attacked you in my e-mail and I'm sorry.

Ross: Fuck off. DON'T CARE WHAT HAPPENS TO EITHER OF YOU.

One month later

Alví: Two months…….ahhhh. No point in calling u. I am sorry for telling Nerissa everything with your dad—that was so wrong. I see it. I didn't think she would say anything to you. I think she hates men, but I know that I should not have told her period. Is there a chance for me to change and prove it? You know, I don't hate you…. Think about you all the time….just like, what you're doin', who has your attention, what you're eating…I can't help it. It feels like you think about me :(

One week later

Alví: Please Ross. Você me completa neste mundo :(:(

In English, this phrase means, "You are the missing piece in my world." It's not that I did not want this work. If anything, I was awe-struck by Alví's relentlessness and courage. I did not have enough life experience to say everything that needed to be said. I was silenced by pride and fear. By Alví saying this phrase in Portuguese, I know he meant it. But I did not identify with Alví's fearless heart yet, nor did I know how to mirror it back in a clear way.

Three weeks later

Alví: I see that you lost your brother. Damn! You know how to reach me if you wanna talk or anything. Praying for the Victorys fa real. I'm so sorry Ross.

Ross: Thank you.

Two hours later

Ross: This may seem random, but I rather write than talk. I should have stayed in Seoul—leaving was a mistake. There was more there than here…and by more I think I mean you. I admit it. For some reason, I thought you wouldn't care if I left or that whatever was happening there was disposable. Idk. I think someone like you is rare.

An hour later

Think hard…is there REALLY space for me with someone like Nerissa? REALLY. Not sure I want to be in a relationship (relationship??) that includes someone like that. Not to disrespect you, but she's damaged. She broke me down and humiliated me to the core. Yo, I did not choose to be bi! Wtf. Easier to be pretend to be gay or straight and just not say anything. I did not choose my dad's actions! I did not choose to meet you…I would not choose any of that!!!!! But Nerissa is the type of woman who will weaponize life to kill off people for herself. Angry and vindictive for no reason. That's not safe.

Minutes later

And…I think that you know and accept that about Nerissa. And I know that's why you didn't introduce us. Protection or something?

Two days later

Ross: Am I right??

Two and half months later

Alví: ROSS, I'm a dad!!!!! Introducing João Carlos Lewis Rio Branco

[pics of Alví and João, and Nerissa and João, attached]

I never cried so hard in my life, wow, wow, wow!

Ross: Why Latin American names so long though? Lol. Are you sure João Carlos' is yours?? WOW, speechless. You did it. You procreated, the world is over, ahhhhhh!

Alví: Hahaha. You can't see his permanent half-smile? Not me?? You know Nerissa's only been with one man— just me.

Ross: LMAO!!!!!!!!!!

Minutes later

Wait! Serious??

An hour later

Ross: Alví, thinkin about João….you're gonna be the best dad. Don't forget to check on him! hold him! Explain to him! Teach him! Cry with him! Don't ever assume his strength and preparation for this world. Teach him how to be better than you. Maybe skip our story, though.

Alví: U know I will 100…wish he could meet u one day. Nah, he'll know everything…if I start with lies and secrets then I already failed. I gotta get this right.

Two years later

Alví: Victory! I'm gonna be in L.A. for the weekend for work. Show me around finally???

A day later

Ross: Alví Rio Branco?! I'm in Thailand right now…

Alví: Of course, you are in THAILAND. Lol

An hour later

Ross: But I leave in two days, stopping in New York…

Alví: Nice. Should we link?

Ross: Same number?

Alví: Nothing has changed :)

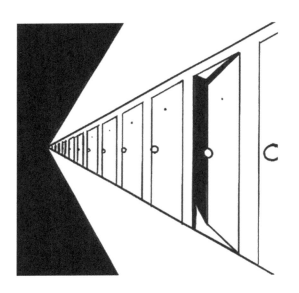

ROOM OF LINGERINGS

It wasn't until I immersed myself in counseling to understand my dad's declining health that I felt the need to also release this story and it's hold on me. To knock and kneel at the doorway of self-reflection on the path and the final step, which millions dread, to peek in and maybe even step inside this room—this room of lingering thoughts and repressed interpretations that had been sprinkled throughout my life, all looking for a *new* source of gravity.

Inside this room there were mirrors. One mirror reflected the need to surrender to mortality and the temporary reality of life by watching my father and brother's death; another mirror reflected the value of moments; another mirror reflected my inner child, who knew a purposeful life instinctually. But a mirror also revealed the deep need to be heard, understood, and upheld and how it felt like to be heard and understood during a moment of escape: Alví.

Although I never saw Alví again (and would have hesitated to meet again), when I dare to look back—when I contemplate diving into the internet abyss and falling into wormholes of obsession about Alví and Nerissa's life on social media—or even when I try to re-create what was lost here, I doubt that this can ever be re-created. Yet I have spent years trying to manifest an Alví 2.0, a Sasha 2.0, and clinging to the rare bisexual unicorns that have crossed my path and make me feel sane. After the night at the club, Sasha disappeared from work and social media. I never saw her again. I learned years later from a co-worker that she died in a hit-and-run accident back home in Oregon. The feelings and thoughts that linger now may or may not be the truth as it occurred then.

During a counseling session, our conversation drifted from my dad to women and men and everything that makes them great and dreadful. We got to the topic of trust—how trust was established, supported, and modeled in my home life. The counselor asked me simply, "Did you trust your dad? Did you trust him to choose you first?" She paused. "How about your mom? Did you trust her to choose you first?"

I was silent during the succession of questions. Her final question was, "Can you tell me one person that you have ever trusted, and with what?" She expounded how the first man and first woman to teach us trust and validation are usually our immediate caretakers, who are typically our biological parents. Learning trust is a foundation block of our development and directly related to the relationships we will have with the waiting sea of penises and vaginas, platonically or romantically. As we age, we will try to fill whatever we lack in all areas of our life for physical and emotional safety. This phenomenon occurs actively and inactively—in warriors, ballerinas, presidents, and homeless people. It happens below the surface and is easy to hide from others on the same journey. I did not realize that this situation with Alví and Nerissa perpetuated an existing (problematic) narrative I had in regard to trusting men and women, with matters of the heart. Being abroad, being unprotected by routine and familiarity amplified inner concerns that were already there. This situation exposed my belief in men and women to cause insurmountable amounts of emotional pain, not only on a platonic level but with all issues of the heart, through humiliation or abandonment.

My counselor told me simply that it "sounds like you and Alví both really, really cared for each other. Did you forgive him?" She paused. "Did you forgive Nerissa?" I asked her repeatedly what she meant by her statement—like I had misheard what she'd said. To me, care is practical—helping someone stand who has fallen; paying for food for someone to eat. But why did I not understand yet that care is also shown through listening. Expressing. Presence through *time* spent with others. I wanted her to validate my suspicions—that being in Seoul somehow had made me more susceptible to Alví. I wanted to hear her say that Alví and Nerissa conjured up a baby to get me out of the picture smoothly. I wanted her to slam down her notebook and tell me to "grow the f*ck up" and learn to separate flings from affection. But none of that was validated.

My counselor patiently described the situational parallels, the repressed needs that stemmed from my childhood expectations of my father and my mother and how social-environmental factors amplified my expectations of men and women and the natural need to seek what I lacked or reject the unfamiliar. "A lot of people go through this Ross, and repress it, but you're doing the work."

It seems apparent that life's journey is more digestible with relationships that encourage, help, and guide. Simply: we need someone to be there, and just maybe they will speak our life language, in which case God has been revealed to us. When I consider Alví next to a "partner" as incompetent as my dad's third wife, Vee, the choosing feels obvious. Physical presence alone does not equal connectedness or necessarily provide value.

LEVEL UP

When I reflect on Alví, my concern is not about force feeding people the nuances of physical biology and soul essence—or even how to access and fill that within myself. Even for the woke, keeping up with the nuances of every experience and preference can be a painstaking process if your daily life does not require that understanding. Being black in America has taught me not to underestimate the power of ignorance or the lack of interest from those who cannot relate or care to relate. I am hesitant to preach that love can occur between the sexes, among the sexes, simultaneously or separately. These are baseline assumptions behind this story. Some may wonder why *this* story? Why now? Why as a book instead of an article or podcast interview? Our country has become grossly distracted by social trends. Weak minds and the impoverished fall prey to messages that are not necessarily invested in their wellbeing.

My responsibility is to communicate *moments that exist in our lives that are taken for granted and prevent self-betterment.* I seek to illuminate the importance of ownership of life experience and self-discovery in order to get to our highest-self quicker. *Views from the Cockpit* + *Panorama* represent the discovery of and experience of inner pain, inner joy, the soul's convictions, approach to sex, and perceptions of the exterior world. These projects embody every aspect of life—the origin, the journey, and the destination.

I often wonder: how do we get to the point where we understand when love *has* occurred in our lives? I ask friends all the time if loss is the *only* way to be present. Sometimes I feel I have missed it and been ignorantly ungrateful. Is trauma the only way to get to the point where we physically understand that love *is* accessible for us and can occur? The loss of my dad has thrown me into a state I never expected to be. For years, I thought of my bisexuality as the bane of my existence until I understood that the bane of existence is, in fact, death itself or living death—a life without purpose. I have shared more than I expected to share. I'm not sure if it's because I instinctively can feel the past holding me back from my best life or if I have lost my damn mind. But it's truth regardless if I share or not. The recovering idealist in me can almost see love in most places now. But then, how do I stay sensitized in a society that callouses? To be clear, I am talking about the occurrence of any shade of affection—platonic, romantic, or paternal. I am talking about the most explicit expressions of companionship—from tantric, sweaty, bareback sex to the most flowerlike and delicate.

Considering human history, in which humanity has never been able to achieve collective empathy as a baseline species trait, I am still drawn to contemplate and reach for a grand, utopian life experience for myself, and wish that for others.

Now that my father has died, I can see his love in most places, even as the degrees of separation occurred. So now I've started the journey to explore all areas and attempt to establish my heart as the authority in my life. Not what I was told or modeled (which has caused the anxiety and disconnect), but authority from my actual life experiences, my sense of self, and my awareness of how the world and people work. As it applies to this story, I believe that sometimes one person holds two keys—one key to unlock our physical selves and the other key to unlock our nonphysical selves. Hold this person tight. Sometimes separate people hold separate keys. Hold them tight. When it's over, all that will matter is our story, the suffering we've endured and what we did next. And I wonder, when you read *Panorama*, in this context, with this packaging, what resonates with you? I hope one idea that crosses your mind is your understanding of people who fall under bi identities. Specifically, bi men who have concluded their identity *consciously* and *studied* which may feel unapparent in overall LGBT progress. Many of whom have faced or are faced with the choice of burning in silence and shame and befriending self-hatred, or risking demonization by asserting their bisexuality (not their actual sexual history).

Bi people in opposite-sex relationships, bis in same-sex relationships, celibate bisexuals, and virginal bisexuals are listening. Transcending the overbearing voices and assumptions feels impossible. I truly believe that truth in all aspects of our life serves to enrich our inner world and the quality of our relationships we attract.

Long ago, I wondered what is a man beside his penis and its ability to impregnate? Not all penises are attached to *men*. Perhaps a man is someone who inherits "land" from his father. Sometimes the land is rich blooming with water lilies and Gazanias. Sometimes it is barren, covered in thorns and toxic soil. But a *man* dares to claim his inheritance and proceeds to pull the weeds of his father's land; he attempts to fertilize and sets *his* stake in the ground to build; he may or may not have athletic ability and emotional intelligence; he may or may not arch his eyebrows and visit a manicurist each month; he may or may not have more female friends than male friends; he may be hung like a whale or have inherited a micro-penis—yet ownership of *his* land is all it takes to stand as a man. Toxic masculinity that some men assert, in fact, is born from a place of borrowed, unclaimed land.

Friedrich Nietzsche, the same philosopher who caused me horror in college, now preaches from the pulpit. In his book, *Thus Spoke Zarathustra*, Nietzsche describes an interesting interaction between a boy and the dragon of "Thou Shalt." The dragon represents all the limitations and burdens set on the boy in the world. In essence, the boy must approach the dragon trembling in fear. The boy breathes in and out rapidly from shock, fading in and out of consciousness, shivering, overcome with bone-deep panic expecting his death by flames. The boy must look into the eye of the dragon of Thou Shalt and say, "I will!" According to the story, the boy must scream it out, he must own these words of "I will" like a lion owns its roar. Only after the boy faces the dragon to proclaim his sovereignty over himself will the dragon reveal itself as an illusion, permitting the boy to assert himself a man.

What will it take for us to look across the deep waters protecting our thought-islands and see ourselves in the shimmering mirage of another? If you see the connections in the stories I have shared, can you also see the bridge between other stories you observe daily? Bridges between rich and poor, black and white, Christian and atheist, American and foreigner, opposite-sex and same-sex, fat and thin, abuse and kindness, Republican and Democrat, healthy and weak, promiscuous and virginal, sane and insane, eloquent and inarticulate? Surely there are bridges everywhere, if only under construction, if only acknowledged. Is humanity itself not a *bridge* between the spirit realms? For the biblically persuaded, was Jesus not the bridge between humans and Father God? Is the process of aging not a bridge, and in essence the most important part of life between birth and death? We know that bridges exist, but for some reason, when the bridge of sexuality is discussed or shown (the overt attraction to men and women), even tactfully, we lose sight of the bridge, at least for some, particularly men. This can only be by design.

People are roaming the Earth for whom God spares no expense on their bodily manifestations. But then some people put God in debt from their investments— not in just their physical appeal, but their heart and their humanity. Some of us can discern that and seek to experience those gifts up-close. Loss has revealed the power fear. Fear is born in the shadow of deceit, and wears a three-piece designer suit in sunlight. Loss also shows the power of surrender and ownership of life experience. If I knew what I know now, I would have applauded Alví's courage in the bar. I would have asked more pressing questions about Nerissa and focused on sustainability. I would have sought to match Alví's courage by communicating explicitly and soulfully. I would have approached Nerissa with compassion to ensure her that I was not a threat, and my intentions considered her.

PANORAMA— THE ESSAY

MEDIA & POLITICS

American media often showcases superficial assertions of what love between humans looks like. Sometimes it's masked in plastic conversations and raunchy, one-dimensional expressions of experience that appear designed to propagate themselves and polarize viewers, listeners, and subscribers for ad clicks. Capitalism teaches us that the more extreme an identity or association can get, the more valid it is, because of its ability to generate money. Identity capitalism. As I wrote, if we look beyond the dynamics of this book into discussions concerning race, class, wealth, political association, and geographic location, we prefer islands—we prefer them unbridged and heavily armored. We prefer walls that block the full panorama of humanity, and the connectedness that we crave for in our loneliest moments. The authentic essence of our humanity does exist on *all* of these islands we prefer, and it can only expand by building and crossing the bridges that separate us.

Why does connection threaten our sense of self? Occurrences of the past deeply damage some of us. Our hearts become calloused. Our ears are deaf. There's a select group of humans who prefer to live and die in an illiterate state. No matter what you show them about any topic or experience. These people tend to occupy positions of authority or associate with authoritative symbols and yield political power. They can easily protect their doublespeak through the oppression and misrepresentation of underrepresented voices.

ROLE OF COMMUNITY

The objective of experiencing life-fulfillment and authenticity is not achieved simply by finding a haven on a secluded island with endless mimosas. Fulfillment is not in a community or group identity that positions itself as exclusive or opposite. The lifeblood of the community comes from *space*—creating spaces and ensuring spaces of togetherness. *Creating* and *providing* are acts of compassion. Real community—undeniable community, semantically and in performance, is born from compassion, giving birth to kindness, which leads to opportunities for unification. Being unified in a collective effort is Step One toward personal fulfillment and freedom.

Societies and communities change—dictionaries are rewritten; people and ideas die off. The point is for us to develop so much that when we outgrow the awareness of the community, we willfully reach back to pull others forward with our knowledge. Having been exposed to both the burgeoning-internet and post-internet era, my generation—millennials—and now Gen Z'ers, can push America into an unrecognizable state by focusing on repairing the shortcomings of generations of the past. We may not be able to blow up the broken systems that have left behind billions, but we have the keen ability to be precise with our language, aligned with our intention, and deliberate with our behavior. Furthermore, we can deeply contemplate if *belonging* or *authenticity* offer more chances at sustained happiness and create space for people to pursue the answer, with the understanding that broken people are broken in a crowded room or alone.

WAR OF WORLDS—THE ITCH

Entertainment through reading is one goal of this missing chapter, but this would not be a real literary work without a strong stance. As a baseline, I want readers to understand that terms like "bi-phobia," "straight pride parades," and "best of both worlds," divide us. For years, I have watched relationships, some up close, some from afar, blow up and disband because of ignorant word-choices and lack of cultural examples. America is, on the one hand, sex-obsessed. On the other, America is completely silent when it comes to men and women, notably men—masculine men—masculine minority men—having the capacity to desire both men *and* women in any variance and what that looks like in the mainstream space. Here is what happens: If two female characters are making out on TV and one goes home to have sex with her husband, she's bi, promiscuous, desirable, or a "tourist." If two men are making out on TV and one goes back to have sex with his wife, he is secretly gay or gay within the shelter of a permitting, self-hating wife. *Where's the variance?*

Semantically, the word *bi-sexual* is misleading. It suggests actual sex is mandatory and implies immediate, simultaneous engagement with men and women. I will upgrade and de-stigmatize this word later.

Someone who chooses to identify as straight or gay and experiences physical or emotional desire to the opposite sex, in some way, at some time, is categorically having a bi experience. This hunger is a psychological need. One either has the desire or not. If the need goes unmet, psychological repression occurs — repression results in self-hate, phobia, and toxic men and women. Mental liberation and perhaps a fulfilling life are possible when desire is satisfied. Frequency and intensity do not invalidate the urge. Most people agree that fulfilment is possible the less internal barriers we have in our lives across the board.

Just as there are loving straight and gay couples who are unable to have sex for some reason physically, there are millions of bisexual virgins. The "confusion" that straight and gay colonizers claim bisexuals experience are <u>because there are no influential cultural templates for bisexuals/ fluid/pansexual people to cling to, nor is their experience politically validated.</u>

Bisexual behavior is depicted and referenced commercially only to be mislabeled, amplifying existing social biases. When a colonizer says, "bisexuality is a phase," "bisexuals are confused," or "bisexuals are not real," the following is what they are saying:

Your bisexuality is cute, but the world I advocate for has limits that I adhere to — being bisexual, fluid, pan, sapio, no label, whatever the f*ck you are, challenges our systems, and the choices I have made personally. You are either gay or straight. Yes, you must decide. A lot of you all kill yourselves from the social isolation and oppression anyway, so maybe repression will be easier for you. Can you afford a therapist? Because you'll probably be angry. We also have church programs that offer conversion. Honestly, I don't care what happens to you. Oh, we will show identifying factors of your experience in every aspect of life because it's actually quite interesting. If you're *a white woman, we will allow you some privilege and admirers. If you're a minority woman, we'll cast you in music videos and movies. If you're a minority man (black, Hispanic, or Asian or heaven forbid an non-English speaking immigrant bisexual)........... probably just kill yourself. We will NEVER permit healthy visibility of your circumstances. Polyamory will never trend, and projections show monogamy increasing as the cost of living goes up. I'll make it easy, which one do most people think you are--straight or gay? Just choose that. Wait, you've never been with man? Why would you think of yourself as fluid, you're straight dummy. For the clever, "woke" ones, if you don't select an option, we will stigmatize your identifier so much that you won't want to associate yourself with anything besides straight or gay anyway—so sorry and best of luck. Oh, the black ones are the cause of HIV...we need them locked up, dead, and unable to procreate. Use what works. God bless.*

For some reason, professed straight women feel threatened; most hate the *idea* of a bi man. The most attractive, "masculine," well-meaning, emotionally skilled bi man can put a woman into anaphylactic shock just from expressing his freedom. A woman's disdain has nothing to do with the man but may occur from her inability to readily discern (and control) the bi man's *sexual* interest in her. Some women have been bold enough to call me disgusting to my face as they run off with their effeminate gay best friend. Before I got control of my ego or understood what was happening, the conversations did not go well. Long, long ago, when I was a teenager, my dad explained to me that p*ssy is power. Many men understand how being a bad husband, or bad boyfriend can manifest into punishment—no access to the p*ssy. If sex is a power structure, is withholding sex effective revenge? What message is implied by a masculine man's sexual power to *want* women and men? Is the fear that he cannot be easily tamed, punished or rewarded?

The divine masculine's role is to ensure the safety and protection of the divine feminine through confidence and clarity for her to feel free and deeply connected to him.

If a bi man harbors fear about disclosure of his identity or if the woman he seeks has reservations about his identity (from stereotypes or otherwise), the bi man is burdened with providing the solution or moving on. For love, he is called to step fully into his masculine energy, and hold space for her needs, to achieve the sense of security and respect both parties desire.

A woman is subject to a world of sexism and also surrounded by the same straight/gay binary messaging that suffocates bisexuals. She may genuinely wonder if a man's bisexuality alone offers her more risk or reward. He may genuinely wonder if the disclosure is worth the effort.

For some reason, gay men find sport in breaking bi men down or fetishizing them. I haven't been able to determine if it's due to jealously—perhaps the word bisexual has a closer association to straight and manliness or if it's from regret—the regret of deciding to repress their own interest in women. Or if it's just to be mean.

It's laughable how real prejudice can be from groups of people we usually associate with soft hearts and in need of social support themselves. History teaches us when people achieve a specific political status, not only do they forget their struggle, but some proceed to torment those behind them. In a perfect world, bi people would live together in ivory towers connected by futuristic glass tunnels, looking down, living, laughing, and dying unphased by a world in disarray.

The cold hard truth is being rejected by *anyone* who does not value authenticity, or at least value curiosity, especially in a dating space, is a colossal gift. Not just in matters of desire. Discovery and curiosity are my core values. And it's been said that rejection is protection. Disclosure to anyone about anything is a choice at all times, and should I *choose* to express myself, I honor my inner child and free up my energy for those best suited to join me on my life journey. Alví taught me that nearly ten years ago. Maybe there will be a day where anyone who suggests they are gay or straight will be *labeled* archaic and extreme, or at least evoke a hearty laugh from the terms' irrelevance to the quest for fulfillment and inner peace.

OSHO, Sasha's favorite philosopher, states, "the body can become a vehicle to that which is beyond the body, and sex energy can become a spiritual force." Perhaps he is referring to a force that is not solely attainable through scientific tests or sexual technique. But a power that is uniquely accessible if identified and understood. All of us possess this "soulful singularity" or "soulful-clarity." Intimacy—real intimacy—is to be equally yoked—mind, body, and spirit. Perhaps biological features are restrictions on the spiritual yoking we seek.

My sense is that sexuality can be a gateway to spirituality. We know other portals to spirituality: prayer, meditation, yoga, service, and fasting. We know making love is different than transactional sex; they both physically feel good, but one feels tremendous. So why isn't sex law of spirituality? Instead of focusing on trite labels and corny, salacious TV scenarios, why are we all not reaching for the profound sense of fulfillment we each are entitled to experience by selection of the proper partner(s)?

WAR OF WORDS: BATTLE OF LABELS & FALSE PROPHETS

While the letter **B** cannot be messily dissociated from LGBTQIA2SP+ and future acronyms that jolt some into reflexive, deadly gags, the **B** experience should never be positioned in mind or state practices as an opposite experience, 50/50 experience, transitional experience or fabricated experience. The proper tactical term to replace the dreadful word **B**i is **B**ridge **B**uilders or those with aBilities. Maybe Sapiosexuals, those who desire intelligence, are Solution-providers. Perhaps **P**ansexuals, those who need emotional connectedness regardless of gender, are **P**romisers. So how about **"BSP"** as the label positioned to encompass every socio-sexual need between absolute straightness and absolute gayness—the **B**ridge **B**uilders, **S**olution-providers, and **P**romisers. **BSP**, I like that. An even more luxurious, disinfected term is—omnisexual.

Even for the strong-willed, the **B** must cope with unique oppression from well-developed, well-funded, bi-phobic opinions, and unchecked stupidity. Misery is perpetuated and quite loud from straights, gays, religious groups, medical care professionals, and the random ignorant stranger that believes them to be a part of a government conspiracy. How does one cope? Tactically, always remember that psychosexual development in all of us requires each developmental stage to be fully resolved. With imperfect people in an imperfect world, complete resolution is not possible. And repression is socially acceptable. Lead with that.

According to the Bisexual Health Resource Center

(www.biresource.org), almost half (40%) of bisexuals have attempted suicide, compared to 25% of gays. For minorities, suicide attempts and mental health statistics are more severe—the details and circumstances are profound. I blame the false prophets who have attached themselves to the perception and symbols of love and acceptance. They have recited scriptures and offered rainbows but have been selective and one-sided with the message of love, focused solely on converting people. I don't understand how spirit exists without a foundational sense of love from *God, the creator*. Ultimately, every child, every teen, every future man, woman or they, no matter their circumstances, must learn how to endure suffering and convert their unique narrative into personal opportunity and resilience. Maybe the community will be there. Perhaps they will resent you. We must develop our arms to be strong enough to lift ourselves.

I propose we dim the rainbow to celebrate (and never lose sight of) real love—born of compassion, supplied by God, the creator, who is incapable of mistakes, but puts us on a quest to discover our purpose in the context of our circumstances. God, the creator—different from the God of a religious text. God who instills a sense of purpose in all things if only to be discovered. Let's smother the cute, cartoon-ish leprechauns who dance in absurdity at the end of the rainbow so that we can refocus the light on the pure color that illuminates us.

I understand the privilege I have to propose and assert such ideas in the form of art. At the same time, governments kill citizens, and churches attempt to alter youth's sexual inclinations through electrocution. Kids and teens who are less headstrong are abused and find themselves living on the street.

I've known I was bi since I was thirteen years old. I didn't hear the term "bi" until I was in college. As a teen, the confusion that adults reference a "bi" or "flip floppy" child may have, for me, occurred from an overpowering, sometimes frightening, awareness. It was not born in turmoil, or a consequence of childhood abuse. I reconciled my identity through years of observation and trial and error. Virginal teenage attraction to women and men were activated separately. Most of my teenage angst around this topic was a result of social invisibility of "the bisexual experience" and the inability to access mindsets and experiences outside of the straight/gay binary.

BSPs, whatever context they are in, can cultivate innate intuition to an overwhelming level if nourished. **BSP**s must understand their plight in a polarized world. Many will find themselves unwelcomed and alone or crowded and alone. If channeled precisely, their intuition can capitalize on direct access to hearts, minds, and, yes, sensual bodies that ache to be touched. Perhaps that is the dangerous message popular culture detects—a fear of the population being accessible to those and abandoned by those who understand and embody unrepressed, uninhibited distinctly male, and distinctly female, deployable energy. Not everyone is asleep about this subject. It was Freud who warned, "In matters of sexuality we are at present, every one of us, ill or well, nothing but hypocrites." Maybe the fear is that **BSP**s reveal the variance of experience related to narrow political agendas and jeopardize the bank accounts of their leadership. Imaginably, the intimidation is that **BSP**s tend to fit gender norms comfortably and are *only* visible when *they* choose to raise their hand, avoiding violence, appearing to skate by the struggle of equality.

WHAT DOES ALL OF THIS MEAN

I am not someone who leads conversations or lives my daily

life with any strong social identity. I don't know if that's due to privilege, elitism, or delusion. From a very early age, I had a sense of myself as a one-person show. I deeply understand now, after losing two people to cancer, that cancer is not just a disease that is a result of physical, genealogical factors. Hurt, repressed and unaddressed truths, guilt, shame, lack of closure, release from events of the past, and inability to forgive, initiate the production of cancer in our mind and emotions. And if sex and affection are a gateway to our spirit and emotions, then the opposite is also exact. The condition of our soul and the fitness of our mind can reveal cancer or vitality in our body.

We know people who will not let one-minute go by without asserting "how Christian they are," "how racist they are," "how gay they are," "how vegan they are," "how macho they are," or "how ethnocentric they are." My favorite are those people who state, "how real they are." These assertions do not begin to reveal their soul's actual convictions and motives. Everyone deserves space, time, and grace, but why are some so quick to assert "their truth" if not only to create an island to protect themselves from alternative thought? Humility and silence feel safer than associating with something imperfect or *almost right*.

NEW STORIES, NEW PRESCRIPTIONS

I don't know the full answer, but I serve with this story. For romantic relationships, perhaps one idea is for us to study monogamy in the modern world and the images of relationships we promote as healthy, honest, sustainable family units. In our circles, we can give grace and space for others to be their best selves. As it applies to **BSPs**, we can be aware not to assume someone is straight, but then not to assume they are gay. "You seem straight," can feel just as awkward as "you seem gay," because of the psychological duality that exists for those in a **BSP** state. Assuming "bi" first, or starting in the center and moving out, neatly creates more space for everyone, and can save a life.

Listen more, speak less.

Productive conversations of sexual relationships will require us to revisit our cultural priorities and to be honest about the scope of human relationships, requiring squeamish, but highly useful discussions.

IDEA # 1: Should we teach little kids in kindergarten spiritual alignment techniques—how to listen for the inner voice and inner truth—to explore and understand their relationship with anger and fear before we line them up for world battle or is reciting scriptures enough? What exactly is the role of education about the intersection of compassion and self-love in the modern world? Do we give kids a counselor to help them understand the dynamics of their specific environment? What does that look like for poor communities? How is access to mental and spiritual resources established when rent is impossible to pay?

IDEA #2: Do we make international-travel or immersive cultural experiences mandatory before high school graduation and create viable systems to fund it?

IDEA #3: Do we expand conversations of sex in childhood education beyond that of abstinence? Do we present appropriately teach psychosexual development as it applies to a child's unique individuality? Do we teach kids that the actual danger of sex is that it puts them in direct touch with the spirit of another person? What if we taught kids that safe sex includes STD-free bodies—yes, but also the careful selection of partners as to ***not absorb, carry, and accumulate the spiritual debris of an unhealed person, which is more disruptive in the long term than an unwanted pregnancy.***

We must honor (or at least respect from a distance) the narratives of those who we perceive to devalue our stories— our race, our manhood or womanhood, and the continuum of gender, our beliefs, our hopes, our dreams. They are due honor with the understanding that *they* are also on a soul-specific journey and the same embodiments of *God, the creator.* We cannot expect grace if we do not understand how to model it, even to those that put our sanity and hearts at risk. For me, this has not come naturally and I try to remember grace by being slow to speak. I've noticed that sharing reveals the common thread of humanity. We all just want to be heard, no matter where we're from, what we've been through or what we've experienced.

FINAL THOUGHT

We all deserve the love that lingers like delicate smoke from a blown-out candle, reaching for heaven. It's the possibility of *this* brand of love, **B**ridge-building love, that reminds me that humans are worth the effort. To feel the blood rushing through our bodies in anger, lust, fear, anticipation, and grief. To feel the blood calm our souls like chamomile tea in a breeze of winter, with soothing acceptance and reassuring patience. We build bridges for those who will walk across and find themselves; we build for those who will discover our path long after we're gone; we share for those who watch us from afar, maybe thinking we have lost our mind, but genuinely cheering on our courage. We build for the one bright-eyed child who does not see themselves in the lineup on TV but understands from our actions that they can be in a future list. I build for J. Ross—a child with unspeakable determination and resolve.

J. Ross, you are heard. You are understood. You are seen and not forgotten.

Let's sail these uncharted waters for sixty years and leave the BS for the philosophers. Let's live so freakin' hard, "they" want to write about us. I'm Ross from Cali. What's your story?

THANK YOU SO MUCH
FOR READING

Share *Views from the Cockpit + Panorama, The Missing Chapter* with a friend, blog about it, review it to share your thoughts about relationships in the 21st century. Be graceful with words to those who appear silent; we never know what people are going through. Lastly, use your awareness of the struggles of **BSPs** and rebuke the notion that their experience is opposite to the political agendas of straight and gay folks. I hope you feel empowered to live *your* best life from *your* view from the cockpit. I dare you to tell your story.

Alví and Nerissa were never heard from again. Both have a large social media presence in their respective industries.

Discussion Questions & Journal Topics

1. Why did the author release this missing chapter?

2. If the author, Alví, and Nerissa were to make amends, what adjustments would you make?

3. Both Alví and the author found themselves in South Korea to escape their home lives. How did escapism shape their relationship? Could this relationship have worked outside of South Korea?

4. How did communication (or lack of communication) shape the events of this story?

5. Which characters perspective would you like to hear more of? Why?

6. Alví takes a significant risk by expressing his interest in the author. What's the most significant risk you've made to tell someone you're interested in them? What was the result? Is there a difference between taking a risk at home as opposed to a foreign place?

7. In the story, the author describes Sasha's biracial

background indicating that Sasha's Korean grand-mother told her it was ok to be black. Why do you think Sasha's grandmother felt the need to give Sasha permission to be black?

8. Why did Nerissa use information about the author's relationship with his father in her message to the author?

9. Should Nerissa and the author have met in Seoul? Why did Alví prevent them from meeting?

10. What are the similarities and differences between the struggles of biracial people and bisexual people?

11. In the book, Alví jokingly asks the author, "Are you going to tell your dad about me?" triggering the author into a defensive response. The author did not write about his religious father's knowledge of his relationship, which occurred at the same time that his father explored *his* sense of belonging and authenticity. Considering what you know of all the characters, how do you think the author's father would have responded to the author and Alví?

12. Why does the author present the acronym **BSP** (and

Omnisexual) to readers and propose disassociating these particular letters from the LGBT+ acronym?

13. There are many TV shows that depict characters that embody opposite sex and same-sex attractions, however characters rarely reference themselves as bi or bisexual. (https://www.thedailybeast.com/the-media-doesnt-know-how-to-talk-about-bisexuality) What is the motivation, if any, of popular culture to erase or misrepresent bi experiences?

14. Suicide and mental health issues are disproportionate among people who identify as bi. Why do you think that is? What is the solution?

15. How can religious groups and LGBT+ groups support people who raise their hands as bi? How have these groups done so far? Why would bi people be called silent majority?

16. The author writes that sexuality is a gateway to spirituality. Considering your personal experiences, do you agree with this statement? How does trans-actional sex and intimate sex shape the conversation surrounding **BSP** experiences?

17. What is more important to you, *belonging*, or *authenticity*?

18. What is the role of monogamy in society?

19. What role does religion play in sexual development? How can sex education be improved in religious settings and grade school with the focus on long-term personal wellness?

20. Is bisexuality a preference (choice), mindset, or lifestyle?

21. Should bi men and women disclose their sexuality when dating? Why or why not? How and when?

ONLINE RESOURCES:

Families and friends with a bi loved-one:

https://bi.org/en/101

Understanding biphobia, bi-invisibility and mental health outcomes:

http://biresource.org/wp-content/uploads/2016/11/
Mental_Health_Biphobia_Brochure.pdf

Bi people of color:

https://www.tandfonline.com/doi/full/10.1080/152997
16.2019.1624121

Bisexuality, theology, and faith-based communities:

http://religiousinstitute.org/projects/bisexuality/

Safe-sex practices for active bi people:

http://www.sexualityeducation.com/pdf/safersexbi.pdf

Is there a link between childhood trauma and adult sexuality? (The author is not a victim of childhood abuse and has listed the link as a resource)

https://www.themeadows.com/blog/
the-impact-of-childhood-sexual-abuse-on-adult-sexuality/

Famous bi people:

https://bi.org/en/famous-bi-people

·

J. Ross Victory (Ross) is an American author, singer/songwriter, and travel enthusiast. He loves music, cars, and serving his local community.

Learn more at
rossvictory.com

Panorama is a stand-alone, but related extension of *Views from the Cockpit: The Journey of a Son*. For the full narrative context and background of the events and characters in Panorama, the author strongly suggests reading the full memoir first.

CPSIA information can be obtained
at www.ICGtesting.com
Printed in the USA
LVHW090600090620
657689LV00012B/1784